The Trail of Tears

The Story of the Cherokee Removal

GREAT JOURNEYS

The Trail of Tears

The Story of the Cherokee Removal

by Dan Elish

BENCHMARK BOOKS

MARSHALL CAVENDISH
NEW YORK

With special thanks to John Bierhorst for his careful review of the manuscript.

Benchmark Books
Marshall Cavendish Corporation
99 White Plains Road
Tarrytown, NY 10591-9001

Cover Photograph: A detail from *Endless Trail*, by Jerome Richard Tiger. Among the
hardships of the forced march was the bitter cold. Many died from exposure.

Photo Research by Candlepants Incorporated
Cover Photo: National Museum of the American Indian, Smithsonian Institution
The photographs in this book are used by permission and through the courtesy of:
National Museum of the American Indian: title page, 14, 53, 63, 70. *Museum of the Cherokee
Indian*: 8, 76, 83. *Smithsonian Institution*: 10, 46, 64. *Corbis*: 24, 36, 38, 89; Bettmann,
16, 21, 29, 50, 80, 91; Marc Muench, 33; Medford Historical Society Collection, 56, 85;
Baldwin H. Ward & Kathryn C. Ward, 60. *Western History Collections, University of
Oklahoma Libraries*: 28, 43, 87 (top), 87 (bottom). *Archives and Manuscripts Division of the
Oklahoma Historical Society*: 41. *Mark Elder*: 67. *Library of Congress*: 79.

Library of Congress Cataloging-in-Publication Data
Elish, Dan.
The Trail of Tears: the story of the Cherokee removal / by Dan Elish.
p.   cm. — (Great journeys)
Includes bibliographical references and index.
ISBN 0-7614-1228-X
1. Trail of Tears, 1838—Juvenile literature. 2. Cherokee Indians—Relocation—Juvenile
literature. [1. Trail of Tears, 1838. 2. Cherokee Indians—History. 3. Indians of North
America—Southern States—History.] I. Title. II. Great journeys
(Benchmark Books (Firm))
E99.C5 E47   2001   973'.04975—dc21   052902

Printed in the United States of America

1 3 5 6 4 2

Contents

Foreword   7

One   Cherokee Civilization   11

Two   The Georgia Rules   25

Three   The Treaty Party   39

Four   Roundup   51

Five   The First Three Groups Go West   61

Six   On the Trail   71

Seven   After the Trail   81

Bibliography   92

Further Reading   94

Index   95

Also by Dan Elish

Fiction

The Worldwide Dessert Contest

Jason and the Baseball Bear

The Great Squirrel Uprising

Born Too Short, Confessions of an 8th Grade Basket Case

Nine Wives (for adults)

Nonfiction

The Transcontinental Railroad

Harriet Tubman

James Meredith

Vermont

Washington, D.C.

Foreword

"Murder is murder, and somebody must answer; somebody must explain the streams of blood that flowed in the Indian country in the summer of 1838. Somebody must explain the four thousand silent graves that mark the trail of the Cherokees to their exile. I wish I could forget it all, but the picture of six hundred and forty-five wagons lumbering over the frozen ground [in the winter of 1839] with their cargo of suffering humanity still lingers in my memory."

—Private John G. Burnett,
Captain Abraham McClellan's Company,
2nd Regiment, 2nd Brigade, Mounted Infantry,
Cherokee Indian Removal, 1838–1839

Private John Burnett, here pictured with Rebecca Moss Burnett, his second wife. "I met and became acquainted with many of the Cherokee Indians," Burnett wrote, "hunting with them by day and sleeping around their campfires by night."

THE CONTINENT OF NORTH AMERICA WAS ONCE FULLY POPULATED BY native tribes, each with its own language and its own rich heritage. These were the people who greeted the earliest European explorers and, later, the first settlers. But the settlers' treatment of the natives they mistakenly called "Indians," makes for one of the most dishonorable chapters in American history. Between the years 1600 and 1900, as settlers pushed westward, Native Americans were repeatedly driven from their homes. Many tribes were forced to give up not only their homelands but their traditional ways of life.

One of the most tragic episodes in this sad history is known as the Trail of Tears. In 1838, sixteen thousand Cherokees were evicted from their homeland in Georgia and forced to relocate to Oklahoma one thousand miles away. Travelling in winter without proper food, clothing, or shelter, four thousand people died en route and had to be buried in shallow, unmarked graves.

"How? How? How could a thing like this happen?"

So asked Private John Burnett, one of the members of the U.S. cavalry who was assigned the task of escorting the Cherokees on their arduous journey.

Undoubtedly, part of the answer to Private Burnett's question lies in the pattern of exploitation and abuse that had been established long before the U.S. government forced the Cherokee from their land. The new settlers could not be bothered to share America's riches with a race of people they viewed as inferior and less "civilized." Ruthlessly expansionist, they had few qualms about conquering a people whose culture was different from their own.

Like any historical drama, the story of the Cherokee removal involved many colorful and outspoken men and women. In recounting the Trail of Tears, I have tried to use as many direct quotes as possible. In this way, I hope to let the main players tell the tragic tale in their own words.

The Three Cherokees, came over from the head of the River Savanna to London 1762.

Native Americans were the source of curiosity ever since Europeans first started coming to the New World. These three Cherokees were sent to England in 1730 to meet King George II.

One

Cherokee Civilization

IN 1838, THE YEAR THE CHEROKEES WERE EVICTED FROM THEIR HOMES, a magazine called the *North American Review* wrote:

> The moment the new world was discovered, the doom of the savage races who inhabited it was sealed; they must either conform to the institutions of the Europeans, or disappear from the face of the earth. . . . Barbarism and civilization were set up, face to face, and one of the other must fall in the encounter. The history of two hundred years is a perpetual commentary upon this text.

Nearly a decade earlier, a writer for the *American Quarterly* had stated:

It has been decreed by Providence, that the civilized and the savage man never shall live for any length of time on the same soil. Either the one or the other must be blotted out of existence.

These two passages are clear examples of a prevailing bias of the early 1800s. Most whites failed to realize that the Native American tribes, the Cherokees in particular, were far from "savage." Quite the opposite was true. The Cherokees were simply civilized in a way the settlers could not understand.

For hundreds, possibly thousands, of years before whites ever set foot in North America, the Cherokees lived in the southern Appalachians, in a sweep of land that extended from North Carolina to South Carolina, northern Georgia, northeastern Alabama, and eastern Tennessee. Just as the Christians believed that God made the heavens and earth in six days, the Cherokee had their own view of creation. According to legend, the Cherokee homeland was created when a water beetle dove to the bottom of the sea and brought up mud that then hardened into ground. Likewise, the mountains and valleys were formed when the great buzzard touched his wings to the soft earth. The Cherokees believed that this homeland made up the center of the world. As a result, they called themselves "Ani-Yun'wiya," or "the principal people." According to Cherokee myth, the first inhabitants of the land were Kana'ti and Selu, their version of Adam and Eve.

Unlike European custom, the mother was the center of the home. Therefore, the typical Cherokee household was comprised of a woman, her husband, her daughters, and their husbands and children. Their villages were situated on riverbanks and centered around the council house, usually a building capable of holding up to several hundred people. There people met to socialize, conduct religious ceremonies, or discuss politics.

Important issues were decided after hours—sometimes days—of debate in which anyone in the village could participate.

Sometimes talk was of war. But the Cherokee never fought for land. Rather, they went to battle to avenge the deaths of other members of the tribe. In the Cherokee religion, it was essential that the world maintain a sense of balance and harmony at all times. If a Cherokee was killed, the world was out of balance until the person responsible for the death had also died. Only then, could the spirit of the dead go to the "darkening land," the Cherokee name for the afterworld. As a result of this belief, Cherokee war parties often had extremely specific goals—to seek revenge on a certain person or a member of that person's family. Once the death had been avenged, the world was back in balance, and the war party would withdraw.

Similarly, this need for balance informed the Cherokee system of justice. The Cherokees had no police and no courts. If a person committed a crime against another, it was up to the injured person and his clan to seek retribution. If someone committed murder, either the murderer or a member of his family had to die. Only then would balance be restored.

The Cherokee quest for harmony pervaded all aspects of their lives. Men hunted in the winter, women planted in the summer. A Cherokee never upset his balance with nature by killing for sport. When a Cherokee hunter killed a deer he apologized to the animal's spirit, explaining that his family needed the food. Once a year, Cherokees attempted to restore order to the world by taking part in the Green Corn Ceremony. At this time houses would be cleaned, old food discarded, and all grievances—except murder—forgiven. Fires would be lit symbolizing renewal. Then the new year would begin with harmony restored.

Because Cherokees only killed when necessary and destroyed their surplus, they didn't acquire wealth. Land was not owned by any single individual but shared by all. Cherokee borders with other Native American tribes weren't even clearly marked. There was an unspoken pact that each

A Cherokee woman gathers corn. In the Cherokee culture, women had enormous power and authority. Not only was family lineage traced through the mother, but women enjoyed a strong voice in village councils.

tribe used only the land that belonged to them. Perhaps it was the lack of importance that the Cherokee attached to money and property that befuddled the Europeans most. Lewis Cass, the governor of the Michigan Territory between 1813 and 1831 and a strong proponent of Cherokee removal, stated the case this way:

> Our forefathers, when they landed upon the shores of this continent, found it in a state of nature, traversed, but not occupied, by wandering hordes of barbarians. . . . There can be no doubt . . . that the Creator intended the earth should be reclaimed from a state of nature and cultivated.

Many whites believed that it had been decreed by God that the vast natural resources of North America should be turned to their advantage. Countless unspoiled acres lay before them, ripe for exploitation. The whites did not share the Cherokee conception of community ownership—a fact to be made all too clear to the Cherokees.

Cherokees and Europeans

THE CHEROKEES FIRST CAME IN CONTACT WITH EUROPEANS IN THE MID-1500s when Hernando de Soto and Juan Pardo, Spanish explorers, came to North America looking for riches—gold, in particular. But instead of the wealthy villages they had hoped to find, the Spaniards came upon Cherokees living modestly off of the land. Unwilling to accept the fact that the natives were not secretly rich, de Soto's soldiers tried to force the Cherokees to show them their gold mines. But how could they lead the Spanish to mines that did not exist? Furious, the Spanish put many Cherokees to death. Others were enslaved. And those natives that were lucky enough to survive found that they didn't possess the natural immunities necessary to fend off a variety of European diseases. As a result,

Spanish conqueror Hernando de Soto confronts a group of Native Americans after crossing the Mississippi River.

thousands of Cherokees succumbed to smallpox, measles, and bubonic plague. The devastation from disease among Native American tribes was so great that some modern historians theorize that in the first 200 years of European presence in North America, 95 percent of the native population died.

Although the Spanish eventually abandoned their fruitless search, it was only the beginning of a wave of European conquest. Beginning in the late seventeenth century, English fur traders began to enter Cherokee territory. It did not take these new Europeans long to infiltrate the Cherokee way of life. Many traders took Cherokee wives. Contrary to Cherokee tradition, these wives lived with their husbands. Likewise, the children of these mixed marriages took their fathers' names and inherited their goods and wealth. Many spoke English and received formal educations. Soon enough, European customs began to influence the Cherokee nation. As the demand for deerskins increased, the Cherokees were forced to rethink their traditional relationship with nature. No longer did they kill only when necessary. They now killed for trade. In 1708, the Cherokees sold 50,000 skins to traders. By 1735 the number approached a million.

By the mid-1700s, the British saw that the native inhabitants could make more than just good trade partners. The whites realized that the natives would be useful allies in their rivalries with other colonists. So the native tribes were recruited and forced to take sides in a variety of European conflicts. The most significant of these was the French and Indian War waged, from 1756 to 1763, between the French and British. Initially, the Cherokees were allied with England. But attacks by English frontiersmen on Cherokee villages soon compelled them to switch sides and join the French. In 1760, Cherokee soldiers defeated a force of 1,600 British at Fort Loudoun in what is now eastern Tennessee. But a year later, the British retaliated, destroying fifteen Cherokee villages, including cornfields and orchards.

In the period between the French and Indian War and the start of the American Revolution in 1775, the British settlers pushed farther into Cherokee territory. Though the British king had delivered a proclamation in 1763 that prohibited settlement west of the Appalachian Mountains, most settlers ignored it and staked claim after claim on Cherokee land. It did not take long for the Cherokees to come to regard this new breed of American colonist as their principal enemy. As a result, when these aggressive settlers decided to fight for their independence, the Cherokees switched their allegiance back to the British.

Needless to say, the Cherokees picked the losing side. As the patriots began to win the revolution, they destroyed Cherokee communities at will, killing most captives on the spot. By the time the war was over, the Cherokees had lost more than fifty villages. Even worse, the Cherokees found themselves on the wrong side of the peace. Years earlier the British Empire had staked its claim to North American soil on what they called the "right of discovery." This was the right the British Empire, as a Christian nation, gave itself to occupy lands inhabited by "uncivilized" people. When the Revolutionary War ended and the Treaty of Paris was signed in 1783, the English conveyed to the young United States all of their rights and claims. Thus, the Indian nations were considered conquered territory, controlled by the newly formed U.S. government.

Unfortunately, a host of individual states began vying for power, and the matter grew more complicated. The southern states of the young America—North Carolina and Georgia in particular—argued that the rights to these "conquered" Cherokee lands belonged to them. In addition, these southern states disregarded the authority of the federal government. In 1783, North Carolina gave its citizens permission to move into Cherokee lands. Georgia, too, allowed settlers to stake claims in native territory. Soon the federal government felt obliged to protect the Indian's interest. The Hopewell Treaty, negotiated in 1785, served as a temporary solution. It read:

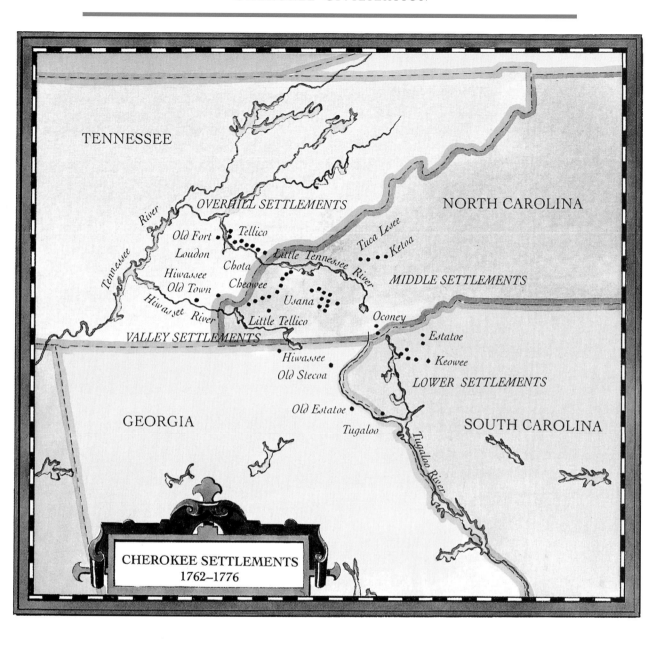

TENNESSEE

OVERHILL SETTLEMENTS

NORTH CAROLINA

River

Old Fort • *Tellico*

Tellico

Tuca Lesee • • • *Ketoa*

Tennessee

Loudon

Little Tennessee River

Chota

Hiwassee
Old Town

Cheowee

MIDDLE SETTLEMENTS

Hiwassee River

Usana

Little Tellico

Oconey

VALLEY SETTLEMENTS

Estatoe

Keowee

*Hiwassee
Old Stecoa*

LOWER SETTLEMENTS

GEORGIA

Old Estatoe

Tugaloo

SOUTH CAROLINA

Tugaloo River

**CHEROKEE SETTLEMENTS
1762–1776**

By the time of the American Revolution, Cherokee territory had been reduced to a series of villages clustered along a network of rivers in the Great Smoky Mountains.

If any citizen of the United States or other person not being an Indian, shall attempt to settle on any of the lands westward or southward of the said boundary which are hereby allotted to the Indians for their hunting grounds, or having already settled and will not remove from the same within six months after the ratification of this treaty, such person shall forfeit the protection of the United States, and the Indians may punish him or not as they please.

On paper, the Hopewell Treaty was an attempt to protect Cherokee holdings. It defined the boundaries of their homeland and gave them the right to expel any intruders. But to some states the treaty held no authority. Georgia and North Carolina continued to insist that the right to the Indian territories lay in the hands of the states, and the federal government backed out of the matter altogether. Though Cherokee tribes did their best to hold onto what was rightfully theirs, the sheer numbers of white settlers quickly became overwhelming.

Still, there was some cause for hope. In the late 1780s the United States was reorganized under the Constitution, which clearly put control of Indian lands in the hands of the federal government. President George Washington appointed Henry Knox, our country's first secretary of war, to implement the government's policy toward natives. Knox believed that the tribes were sovereign, independent nations and that the United States should recognize their rights. But he also believed in what he called "expansion with honor," a policy that held that as America grew, the Indians had to give over some of their lands to accommodate the growing white population. His hope was that the natives would ultimately adopt European ways and eventually blend in with the culture that had slowly come to dominate rural America.

His first order of business was passing the first Indian Trade and Intercourse Act in 1790. This law gave the federal government the power

Henry Knox, the first U.S. secretary of war. He believed that America's native residents were capable of becoming "civilized" and that they would embrace the white culture that came to dominate the newly independent nation.

to negotiate treaties with tribes. Realizing that many settlers had already moved illegally onto native land, Knox then negotiated the Treaty of Holston in 1791. In this treaty, new boundaries were drawn yet again, diminishing Cherokee holdings. More importantly, the federal government pledged to help the Indians keep new settlers off their land.

But the promises were never kept. Between 1776 and 1794, the Cherokees were forced to surrender more than twenty thousand miles of their territory. As time passed, many Cherokees began to object to the cycle of ceding more and more land in return for more treaties. From 1684 to 1819, the Cherokees had signed twenty eight of them! In 1817, a council of Cherokee women decided that they had had enough and circulated a series of petitions to the Cherokee National Council—the main governing body—urging them not to give up any more land:

Your mothers, your sisters ask and beg of you not to part with any more of our land. . . . But keep it for our growing children, for it was the good will of our creator to place us here, and you know our father, the great president [at that point, James Monroe], will not allow his white children to take our country away.

Despite the efforts of the Cherokee women, more treaties were signed. In 1819, the Cherokees ceded 989,880 acres of mountain land in North Carolina, 536,000 acres in Georgia, 739,000 acres in Alabama, and 1,541,100 acres in Tennessee. Although this was a terrible blow to the tribe, one Cherokee sympathizer, Reverend Samuel Worcester, seemed to think that, given what they were up against, the Indians had gotten a better deal than they could have expected. He wrote to Hicks, a Cherokee chief:

You feared that you would be compelled to give up your houses, your cornfields, your rivers, plains and mountains. . . . The dark cloud has passed away. A good portion of your lands is secured to you; the wicked men who seek your hurt are to be kept from troubling you. You are to be allowed to sit quietly around your own fires and under your own trees and all things are to be set before you and your children. . . . Brother, it is the morning of a new and happy day.

Samuel Worcester, though good hearted, was nevertheless suffering from a severe case of wishful thinking. As badly as the Cherokees had been treated since the mid-1540s, it was about to get even worse.

A rendering of a Cherokee "warrior" from the early nineteenth century. He is referred to as the "commander in chief" of his nation. Such portrayals of Native Americans were hardly accurate, but reflected instead European notions of culture and refinement.

Two

The Georgia Rules

All I want in this Creation
Is a pretty little wife and a big plantation
Way up north in the Cherokee nation.

—popular song in Georgia in the 1820s

IN ORDER TO FULLY UNDERSTAND THE PROBLEMS FACED BY THE CHEROKEE Nation in the 1820s, it is necessary to look back twenty years to the beginning of the century. In 1802, Thomas Jefferson, then the third president of the United States, negotiated an agreement in which the state of Georgia agreed to "relinquish" its claim to lands—acreage it never rightfully owned—extending west of the Mississippi River. In return, Georgia would receive money along with a promise "as early as the same can be peaceably obtained, on reasonable terms," that the federal government would nullify Cherokee and Creek Indian claims within the state's borders.

It was this agreement that, more than anything, gave Georgia the leverage it needed to eventually force the Cherokees from their homeland. But although this agreement was struck in 1802, the issue didn't come to a head until the 1820s. For it was during that decade that it became clear the Cherokees were, indeed, becoming "civilized" and thereby strengthening their hold on their homeland.

For many years, it was the desire of well-intentioned whites that the native tribes adopt European customs and work their way into the American mainstream. In July 1791, the Treaty of Holston solidified this hope that "the Cherokee nations may be led to a greater degree of civilization, and to become herdsmen and cultivators, instead of remaining in a state of hunters."

The wish was that the Indians would reject their traditional notions of communal ownership of land and property and embrace the American ideals of free enterprise. In short, the Cherokee should be molded into businessmen. In 1838, the year the Cherokees were forced from their homes, the commissioner of Indian affairs stated, "Common property and civilization cannot co-exist." And a report by another Indian commissioner asserted that the native must "be imbued with the exalting egotism of American civilization, so that he will say 'I' instead of 'We,' and 'This is mine,' instead of 'This is ours.'"

Toward the beginning of the nineteenth century, many Cherokees made an effort to embrace the American system of free enterprise. Some Cherokee planters acquired slaves and raised cotton. Others opened stores and taverns or operated ferries or toll roads. In order to address the growing disparity of wealth among Cherokees, the tribe passed its first recorded law in 1808, which established a police force. Soon enough, there were other laws on the books, mostly dealing with owning property. In 1810 a law was passed that took the right to avenge death out of the hands of the Cherokee clans and gave it to the U.S. government. In

1817, another law gave the National Council the right to cede lands. In 1827, the Cherokees adopted a constitution, complete with a chief executive, congress, and judicial system. In fact, the preamble to the Cherokee constitution read much like the one to the U.S. Constitution.

By 1826, the people of the Cherokee Nation reportedly owned 22,000 cattle, 7,600 horses, 2,500 sheep, 46,000 swine, 2,488 spinning wheels, 762 looms, 2,948 plows, 1,277 slaves, 172 wagons, 10 sawmills, 31 gristmills, 62 blacksmith shops, 8 cotton machines, 18 ferries, miles of road, and 18 schools—all in all, quite a prosperous nation.

The census of 1835 demonstrates clearly that many Cherokees were doing well by any standard. For instance, there was James Vann, a landowner with fourteen slaves, a hundred acres, and twenty houses. Of special note is the fact that in the James Vann household were two Cherokees who could read English. For despite their economic successes, many Americans felt strongly that the only way for the native population to fully fit into American life was to learn English. In 1822, Indian agent Jedediah Morse, wrote these words to the U.S. secretary of war:

Let the Indians forget their own languages, in which nothing is written, and nothing of course can be preserved, and learn ours, which will at once open to them the whole field of every kind of useful knowledge. . . . Let the Indians of our country be taught to read and speak the English language, and it will effect more towards civilizing and christianizing them than all human means besides.

Though most Cherokees spoke English and some, like James Vann, could even read it, the tribe refused to let their rich native tongue become a dead language. In 1821, Sequoya, a Cherokee known to whites as George Guess or Gist, perfected a syllabary, or alphabet, which allowed Cherokees to read and write their own language. Though Sequoya's syllabary had eighty-five letters, it was extremely easy to learn due to the fact

A painting of David Vann, a member of one of the most prosperous Cherokee families. Many poor whites were deeply resentful of successful Cherokees.

that each character had only one sound. In fact, many Cherokees who had been illiterate learned to read and write in Cherokee in a matter of days. As a result of Sequoya's remarkable achievement, on February 21, 1828, the *Cherokee Phoenix*, a four-page weekly newspaper, printed in both Cherokee and English, began publication in New Echota, Georgia.

Soon the Cherokees' adoption of the customs and trappings of white society was too obvious to be ignored. Sally M. Reece was a missionary who taught at a school on the Cherokee homelands. She wrote in 1828:

Sequoya with a tablet of the syllabary it took him ten years to create. His alphabet transformed the Cherokee Nation into a fully literate society practically overnight.

First I will tell you about the Cherokees. I think they improve. They have a printing press, and print a paper which is called the Cherokee Phoenix. They come to meeting on Sabbath days. They wear clothes which they made themselves. . . . They keep horse, cows, sheep, and swine. Some have oxen. They cultivate fields. They have yet a great many bad customs but I hope all these things will soon be done away. They have thought more about the Saviour lately. I hope this nation will soon become civilized and enlightened.

Of course, a "civilized and enlightened" Cherokee Nation was the last thing the state of Georgia wanted. After all, well-educated, English-speaking Cherokees were difficult to intimidate especially when many of them shared the same economic values as their white neighbors. It became nearly impossible for a poor Georgian farmer to point to a rich Cherokee and say that God intended "uncivilized Indians" to give up their land to the "civilized" whites.

The biggest turning point, however, came in 1827 when the Cherokees adopted their own constitution. Georgians were furious that the Cherokees would have the gall to not only define the borders of their nation but to claim the right to govern within those boundaries. Then in 1828, gold was discovered in Cherokee territory. Seemingly overnight, communities of white claim jumpers, eager for their share, rose up. As one reporter wrote, "The dust became a medium of circulation, and miners were accustomed to carry about with them quills filled with gold."

John Burnett, the private in the U.S. Army, who escorted the Cherokees west, put it this way:

In the year of 1828, a little Indian boy living on Ward Creek (Tennessee) had sold a gold nugget to a white trader, and that nugget sealed the doom of the Cherokees. In a short time, the country was over run with armed brigands claiming to be Government Agents, who paid no attention to the rights of the Indians who were the legal possessors of the country. Crimes were committed that were a disgrace to civilization. Men were shot in cold blood, lands were confiscated. Homes were burned and the inhabitants driven out by these gold-hungry brigands.

The people of the state of Georgia began to do whatever they possibly could to expel the Cherokees. In 1826 and 1827 the Georgia general

Blacks on the Trail

The Cherokees, of course, were a nation of people who were systematically harassed and persecuted by whites. It is ironic then that in the 1820s, as the tribe grew more "civilized," many wealthier Cherokees acquired slaves.

By all accounts blacks were generally treated more humanely within the Cherokee Nation than they were on farms and plantations elsewhere in the South. Many people living in the territory were abolitionists, men and women who believed slavery should be abolished. In fact, by 1835 a strong movement was afoot to emancipate the slaves and make them Cherokee citizens. Unfortunately, that plan was derailed when the Treaty Party signed the Treaty of New Echota.

Many blacks made the sad trek west on the Trail of Tears. One Cherokee remembered, "My grandparents were helped and protected by very faithful Negro slaves who . . . went ahead of the wagons and killed any wild beast who came along." Historians estimate that of the approximately 4,000 people who died in the army stockades and on the trail, as many as one-quarter were black.

Indeed, the "trail where we cried" contained not only the tears of grieving Cherokees, but of black men and women as well.

assembly passed resolutions that stated that by virtue of its colonial charter, Georgia held sovereign dominion over all peoples within its borders. Further, if the United States failed to honor the agreement of 1802 and acquire the Cherokee Nation, the state had the right to simply take it. In 1828, the Georgia legislature stated:

> The policy which has been pursued by the United States toward the Cherokee Indians has not been in good faith toward Georgia. . . . That all the lands, appropriated and unappropriated, which lie within the conventional limits of Georgia belong to her absolutely; that the title is in her; that the Indians are tenants at her will.

But Georgia wasn't content to stop there. In December 1829, the state assembly passed a law that read, in part:

> After the first day of June next, all laws, ordinances, orders and regulations of any kind whatever, made, passed, or enacted by the Cherokee Indians, either in general council or in any other way whatever, or by any authority whatever of said tribe, be, and the same are hereby declared to be null and void and of no effect.

In addition, the Georgians passed a law that made it illegal for a Cherokee to dig for gold within the state of Georgia.

But did these laws have an effect on the Cherokees? Not really. If anything, Georgia's sudden fierce desire to get rid of them strengthened their resolve. In the autumn of 1829, the National Council passed a resolution that stated if any Cherokee "should treat and dispose of any lands belonging to this nation without special permission from the national authorities, he or they shall suffer death."

In short, Georgia and the Cherokee Nation had reached an impasse. There would be no easy resolution to the escalating tensions. Georgia

What all the fuss was about: a vast tract of land the Cherokees refused to give up. Today part of this hotly contested acreage has been turned into the Cherokee National Forest in Tennessee.

was unrelenting in its continued efforts to expel the Cherokees. Luckily for Georgia's government officials, they now had a strong ally in the White House. Elected president in 1828, Andrew Jackson had achieved great acclaim as an Indian fighter. Ironically, he had made his reputation in 1814 fighting with the Cherokees against the Creek Indians. Even so, Jackson was not partial to any group of Indians. Upon entering office, he lobbied intensively for their relocation to the West. Siding with Georgia, he argued that the U.S. Constitution forbade one state to exist within the borders of another. The Indians, then, could either "emigrate beyond the Mississippi or submit to the laws of those States [Georgia]." This viewpoint made Jackson the first president who recognized Georgia's claims to Cherokee land. In 1829, he proposed the Indian Removal Act, a law that would provide Congress with the funds to buy tribal lands and give the president authority to move the tribes west. Many northerners opposed the measure. Vermont representative Horace Everett proclaimed, "The evil . . . is enormous; the violence is extreme; the breach of public faith deplorable; the inevitable suffering incalculable." But despite such strenuous objections, the bill passed by four votes and became law. Some years later, Chief Junaluska, a man who had saved Jackson's life in the battle against the Creeks in 1814, said, "If I had known Jackson would drive us from our homes I would have killed him that day at the Horse Shoe." But Jackson saw things differently. In his State of the Union address of 1830 he asserted:

Rightly considered, the policy of the General Government toward the red man is not only liberal, but generous. He is unwilling to submit to the laws of the States and mingle with their population. To save him from this alternative, or perhaps utter annihilation, the General Government kindly offers him a new home, and proposes to pay the whole expense of this removal and settlement.

But the Cherokees refused to budge. In return, Georgia applied additional pressure, coming up with more laws engineered to make the Cherokees miserable and drive them from their homes. A law that went into effect in February 1831 required all whites living within the Cherokee Nation to take an oath of allegiance to the state of Georgia. Any white man caught living within Cherokee borders could be subject to four years of hard labor. Further, Georgia's government divided Cherokee land into lots and gave it away to white Georgians by lottery.

It was outrageous treatment. To their credit, the Cherokees did not resort to violence in their efforts to stop Georgia from stripping them of their rights. Rather, they challenged Georgia in the U.S. Supreme Court.

The first case to reach the court was *Cherokee Nation v. Georgia* in 1831. In this case, the Georgia guard had arrested a Cherokee citizen, George Tassel, for murdering another Cherokee within the Cherokee homeland. Rather than let the Cherokee system of justice deal with the case, the Georgia state government executed Tassel. Of course, the Cherokees felt that their state should have had the right to try and sentence Tassel. Although Chief Justice John Marshall wrote, "If courts were permitted to indulge their sympathies, a case better calculated to excite them can scarcely be imagined," he ruled in favor of Georgia, stating that the Cherokee Nation had no legal standing as a "foreign nation." Though disappointed, the Cherokees won a momentous decision a short year later. This time, Samuel Worcester, a missionary working in Cherokee territory, was arrested for refusing to take an oath pledging his allegiance to the state of Georgia. In this case, *Worcester v. Georgia*, Chief Justice Marshall wrote:

The Cherokee Nation, then, is a distinct community, occupying its own territory, with boundaries accurately described in which

The Cherokees found no friend or advocate in the newly elected president Andrew Jackson. Considered a military hero, some Americans admired him for his ruthless slaughter of Indians in the South.

the laws of Georgia can have no force and which the citizens of Georgia have no right to enter, but with the assent of the Cherokees themselves.

Then Justice Marshall went even further, writing, "The acts of Georgia are repugnant to the Constitution, treaties and laws of the United States."

The Cherokees had realized a minor victory. Unfortunately, it soon became clear that Andrew Jackson had no intention of using the power of the federal government to enforce the high court's decision.

"John Marshall has made his decision," he said. "Now let him enforce it."

With those words, the Cherokee Nation drew one step closer to its forced removal.

John Ross, chief of the Cherokee Nation from 1828 until his death in 1866. A tireless proponent of the Cherokee's right to stay in the East, Ross wrote in 1836, "I still strongly hope we shall find ultimate justice from the good sense of the administration and of the people of the United States. . . . The Cherokees . . . have no weapon to use but argument."

Three

The Treaty Party

In the years leading up to the Trail of Tears, the Cherokee Nation was fortunate enough to have a worthy leader named John Ross. Born in 1790 of a Scottish father and a mother who was part Cherokee, Ross was raised as a Cherokee, even though he was sent to white schools, most notably Kingston Academy in Tennessee. During the War of 1812, he attained the rank of major and served under future president Andrew Jackson. Soon thereafter, Ross proved himself in the world of business and rose rapidly through the Cherokee ranks. Elected to the Cherokee National Committee in 1817, he became its president two years later. After helping draft the Cherokee Constitution, he was named chief in 1828, a post he held until his death in 1866.

Throughout his career, Ross was a vocal opponent of relocation and enjoyed the support of the majority of the Cherokee Nation until the time of removal in 1838. But when it became clear that President Jackson had no intention of enforcing the Supreme Court's 1832 decision, some Cherokees began to see removal as inevitable. This vocal minority came to be known as the Treaty Party. Its leader was a man named Major John Ridge. A successful planter, Ridge was considered the most eloquent speaker in the Cherokee National Council. A true patriot, he was responsible for passing a law that made selling any Cherokee land punishable by death. Even so, Ridge felt that the Cherokees should move west while they still had a "choice." His son, John Ridge, agreed with him. The Cherokee people, he said "were robbed and whipped by the whites almost every day." With President Jackson refusing to protect the Cherokee people and the Georgia government doing whatever it could to make their lives miserable, why put up with it?

The Treaty Party grew in support and soon found the perfect spokesman in Elias Boudinot, a cousin of John Ridge and editor in chief of the *Cherokee Phoenix*. As the tribe's situation steadily worsened, Boudinot's editorials lashed out at the state of Georgia and the federal government. As he wrote in 1831,

> Will the Congress of the United States permit its citizens to invade us in a warlike manner in time of peace . . . . I do conscientiously believe it to be the duty of every citizen to reflect upon the dangers with which we are surrounded; to view the darkness which seems to lie before our people, our prospects, and the evils with which we are threatened; to talk over all these matters, and, if possible come to some definite and satisfactory conclusion.

Later editorials became more inflammatory. Although John Ross believed in freedom of the press, he could not allow the only Cherokee newspaper to become a mouthpiece for those few Cherokees who wanted to give in to the government's pressure. As a result, Ross forced

Elias Boudinot, editor of the Cherokee Phoenix, *eventually joined the Treaty Party. A man of strong opinions, he aided missionaries in what he felt was the essential task of translating the Bible into the Cherokee language.*

Boudinot to resign the editorship and replaced him with his son-in-law Elijah Hicks.

A few days after his dismissal, Boudinot wrote a final editorial for the *Phoenix* in which he defended his own patriotism and laid out the case for moving the tribe west.

In applying the above definition of patriotism to my conduct, I can but say that I have come to the unpleasant and most disagreeable conclusion . . . that our lands, or a large part of them, are about to be seized and taken from us. Now, as a friend of my people, I cannot say *peace, peace*, when there is no peace. I cannot ease their minds with any expectation of a calm, when the vessel is already tossed to and fro, and threatened to be shattered to pieces by an approaching tempest. If I really believe there is danger, I must act consistently, and give alarm; tell our countrymen our true, or what I believe to be our true, situation. In the case under consideration, I am induced to believe there is danger, "immediate and appalling," and it becomes the people of the country to weigh the matter rightly, act wisely, not rashly, and choose a course that will come nearest to benefiting the nation.

Although today Boudinot's warnings seem well within the realm of reason, in his time, most Cherokees viewed them as traitorous. Yes, the Georgia and federal governments were making a peaceful life seemingly impossible. But how could a true Cherokee really consider leaving? As a result, the overwhelming majority of citizens continued to side with John Ross and decided to wait out the Jackson presidency in the hopes that the Cherokee Nation could strike a deal and remain in their homeland. Ross worked tirelessly. Time after time, he traveled to Washington, D.C., to meet with the president, negotiate treaties, and to do whatever he could to stave off the inevitable. But Ross was unable to rally the support he needed. He could not get the federal government to enforce the decision of the Supreme Court that had given the Cherokees the right to their own nation within the state of Georgia. And in the process, Ross himself paid a high price. When the Georgia government began to possess the property of some of the wealthier Cherokees, he was thrown out of his own home.

Despite everything, John Ross never gave up. But as the Treaty Party kept up the pressure to move the tribe west, Ross agreed to meet with the Ridges and Boudinot at Red Clay, Tennessee. Unfortunately, the two sides could not agree. Instead, the chiefs who opposed removal chose a

Major Ridge, leader of the Treaty Party, is a complex figure in the history of the Cherokee. Considered a traitor by many of his people, he felt he had no choice and that giving up the land saved the lives of countless Cherokees.

delegation to travel to Washington to appeal once again for relief from the unjust treatment they were receiving. Unwilling to sit on the sidelines, the Treaty Party sent its own delegation to Washington as well. President Jackson skillfully played the two sides off of each other. Forced into negotiating, Ross agreed to present a proposed treaty outlining the federal government's demands before the Cherokee Council in 1835. But the Cherokee Council flatly rejected this treaty. The majority of Cherokees still had no intention of exchanging their land for money.

That is when the U.S. treaty commissioner, John F. Schermerhorn, became involved and called for a new conference at New Echota, Georgia, in December 1835. Since Ross was on yet another trip to

Washington to attempt to negotiate a workable agreement with the federal government, he was unable to attend. His absence proved to be badly timed. For Major Ridge and the members of the Treaty Party took the opportunity to negotiate a treaty with the United States in which the Cherokees agreed to cede the remainder of their homelands and move west. Clearly, this Treaty of New Echota didn't represent the will of the majority of the Cherokee people. In fact, out of a population of about 16,000, only two hundred Cherokees were in New Echota to vote! Even so, the U.S. Senate ratified the treaty in 1836. Now Andrew Jackson had the document he had been looking for. The Cherokees had agreed to move. In return for their sacred homelands, the Cherokees would receive safe passage west along with money to be allotted as follows:

For Removal	$ 255,000
Subsistence	$ 400,000
Improvements and ferries	$1,000,000
Claims and spoilations	$ 250,000
Domestic animals	$ 10,000
National debts	$ 60,000
Public buildings	$ 30,000
Printing press, etc.	$ 5,000
Blankets	$ 36,000
Rifles	$ 37,000
Kettles	$ 7,000
Per captita allowance	$1,800,000
General fund	$ 400,000
School fund	$ 160,000
Orphan's fund	$ 50,000
Additional territory	$ 500,000
Total	$5,000,000

But in the end, it was the government that got the best deal. They had purchased the Cherokee homeland for five million dollars.

John Ross was furious. He wrote in 1836:

I must distinctly declare to you that I believe, the document [Treaty of New Echota] signed by unauthorized individuals at Washington, will never be regarded by the Cherokee nation as a Treaty. . . . I still strongly hope we shall find ultimate justice from the good sense of the administration and of the people of the United States.

Many Americans—especially in the North—shared Ross's outrage. Some of the most respected intellectuals in the country supported the Cherokee cause. Upon hearing of the fraudulent treaty, Ralph Waldo Emerson, one of the country's most famous writers, quickly dispatched a letter to the newly elected president, Martin Van Buren:

Such a dereliction of all faith and virtue, such a denial of justice, and such deafness to screams for mercy were never heard of in times of peace and in the dealings of a nation with its own allies and wards, since the earth was made.

Sir, does this government think that the people of the United States are become savage and mad? From their minds are the sentiments of love and a good nature wiped clean out? The soul of man, the justice, the mercy that is that heart's heart in all men, from Maine to Georgia, does abhor this business.

Still other Americans were saddened by the Cherokee plight. Henry Clay of Kentucky, one of the foremost senators of the era, noted:

Even the lot of the African slave is preferable, far preferable to the

purpose as soon after the ratification of this Treaty as an appropriation for the same shall be made. It is however not intended in this Article to interfere with that part of the Annuities due the Cherokees west by the Treaty of 1819.

Article 19 This treaty after the same shall be ratified by the President & senate of the United States shall be obligatory on the Contracting parties.

In testimony whereof the Commissioner and the Chiefs head men & people whose names are hereunto annexed being duly authorized by the people in general Council assembled have affixed their hands & seals for themselves & in behalf of the Cherokee Nation. I have examined the foregoing treaty and altho' not present when it was made, I approve its provisions generally and therefore sign it.

Cue te hee his mark (Seal)

Te gah e ska his X mark (Seal)

J. F. Schermerhorn (Seal)

Robert Rogers (Seal)

Major his X Ridge mark (Seal)

John Gunter (Seal)

James his X Foster mark (Seal)

John A. Bell (Seal)

Tesa Taeskey his X mark (Seal)

Charles F. Foreman (Seal)

Charles his X moore mark (Seal)

William Rogers (Seal)

George his X Chambers mark (Seal)

George W Adair (Seal)

Jah yeske his X mark (Seal)

Elias Boudinot (Seal)

Archilla his X Smith mark (Seal)

James his X Starr mark (Seal)

Andrew Ross (Seal)

Jesse Halfbreed his X mark (Seal)

William Lasley (Seal)

condition of this unhappy nation. The interest of the master prompts him to protect his slave: but what mortal will care for, protect the suffering injured Indian, shut out from the family of man?

But even though the majority of the Cherokees thought that the Treaty Party had betrayed them, Elias Boudinot remained firm. In 1837 he issued a general reply to John Ross that once again stated why he felt that the Treaty Party had taken the only logical course.

Removal, then, is the only remedy, the only practicable remedy. By it . . . our people may rise from their very ashes, to become prosperous and happy, and a credit to our race. . . . What is the prospect in reference to your plan of relief, if you are understood at all to have any plan? It is dark and gloomy beyond description. Subject the Cherokees to the laws of the States in their present condition? It matters not how favorable those laws may be, instead of remedying the evil you would only rivet the chains and fasten the manacles of their servitude and degradation. The final destiny of our race, under such circumstances, is too revolting to think of. Its course must be downward, until it finally becomes extinct or is merged in another race, more ignoble and more detested.

In the end, the majority of the Cherokees were not swayed by Boudinot's arguments and stood by John Ross to the end. In their eyes the Treaty of New Echota was a travesty and a fake. As Ross himself wrote to a friend in 1836:

The signature page of the Treaty of New Echota. Though only supported by a minority of the Cherokee people, the U.S. government used this treaty as their legal claim to completing the removal.

William Penn

Jeremiah Evarts was a missionary who was outraged at the treatment of the Cherokees. Between August 5 and December 19, 1829, under the pseudonym William Penn, Evarts wrote twenty-four separate articles entitled, "Essays on the Present Crisis in the Condition of the American Indian." Reprinted in newspapers across the country, Evarts' "William Penn" essays were a direct response to Andrew Jackson's proremoval policies and became perhaps the most important pieces of pro-Indian propaganda in the country. The following is an excerpt from one of his many powerful essays.

Is it true, that while treaties are declared in the constitution to be the supreme law of the land, a whole volume of these supreme laws is to be at once avowedly and utterly disregarded? Is the Senate of the United States, that august body, as our newspapers have called it a thousand times, to march in solemn procession, and burn a volume of treaties? Are the archives of state to be searched, and a hundred and fifty rolls, containing treaties with the Indians, to be brought forth and consigned to the flames on Capitol Hill, in the presence of the representatives of the people, and all the dignitaries of our national government? When ambassadors from foreign nations inquire, *What is the cause of all this burning?* are we to say, "Forty years ago President Washington and the Senate made treaties with the Indians, which have been repeated and confirmed by successive administrations. The treaties are plain, and the terms reasonable. But the Indians are weak, and their white neighbors will be lawless. The way to please these white neighbours is, therefore, to burn the treaties, and then call the Indians our dear children, and deal with them precisely as if no treaties had ever been made." Is this answer to be given to the honest inquiries of intelligent foreigners? Are we to declare to mankind, that in our country law is totally inadequate to answer the great end for which human laws are made, that is, the protection of the weak against the strong? And is this confession to be made without feeling and without shame?

I wish I could acquiesce in your impression, that a Treaty has been made, by which every difficulty between the Cherokees and the United States has been set at rest; but I must candidly say, that I know of no such Treaty.

Though Ross and his followers had right on their side, the federal government had the might. Struck under questionable circumstances, the Treaty of New Echota would be enforced nonetheless. The Cherokees would move west.

This log cabin on the Qualla Reservation in North Carolina was typical of Cherokee dwellings from the 1830s.

Four

Roundup

YEARS OF CRUELTY ON THE PART OF THE GEORGIA GOVERNMENT HAD taken its toll on the Cherokee. Many families had already been thrown out of their homes and stripped of their means of livelihood. Now the crowning defeat, the Treaty of New Echota, gave the Cherokees two years to move to Indian Territory in the present state of Oklahoma.

But, with the plan for removal secured, did the Georgia government relax its efforts to drive out the Cherokees? Not at all. If anything, the state became even more underhanded in its attempts to control the natives and their lands. For instance, the Cherokee Nation had strict laws forbidding the sale of alcohol. But the Georgia government suspended these measures, leading to a flock of whiskey traders invading Cherokee territory. Demoralized by years of mistreatment, in search of relief, some Cherokees turned to the once-banned liquor. Even worse, many were forced to enroll for removal—and thereby give up their rights to the land—while they were drunk. On June 22, 1836, the Cherokee tribe sent this letter of protest to the U.S. House of Representatives describing Georgia's cruel tactics:

Atalah Anosta was prevailed upon to enrol when drunk, contrary to the wish and will of his wife and children; when the time arrived for him to leave for Arkansas, he absconded. A guard was sent after them. . . . which arrested the woman and children, and brought them to the agency about dark, in a cold rain, shivering and hungry. They were detained under guard all night, and part of the next day, and until the woman agreed to enrol her name as an emigrant. The husband then came in, and he and his wife and their children were put on board a boat and taken to Arkansas.

Of course, for every Cherokee family forced from its home, a white one was waiting to take its place. Zillah Haynie Brandon was among the newcomers, settling in Cherokee territory in 1828. Years later, as an elderly woman, she wrote a memoir. Though she holds to many traditional stereotypes of the "savage Indian," Brandon does describe the state of desolation that ran throughout the Cherokee community as removal loomed.

In sixty yards of our house there lived three families of Indians, who like their whole tribe, looked as if the very shafts of desolation was hanging around them. . . . The women I believe were chaste and very civil, but their husbands would drink to drunkenness, and were very cruel when under the influence of the fire water.

When they were sober, we were not afraid of them, but their drinking was so common a thing, a whiskey shop being kept by a white man in a quarter of a mile of us, that it was impossible to tell when we were safe. . . . They [Cherokee men] would stand outside

Cherokee men on the eve of removal. John Ridge wrote in an 1836 letter to President Jackson, "A great many of the Cherokees have been disarmed of their rifles by the Georgians . . . greatly to the injury of the Indians, as they are in a wretched condition for food."

of their houses weeping and looking so doleful, that it would move any heart, not possessed of a demon, to pity.

The proud Cherokees had indeed become bereft of hope. Outraged at the situation, General John Ellis Wool, inspector general of the U.S. Army who had been ordered in July 1836 to take command of federal troops in the Cherokee Nation, resigned his post when President Jackson left office in 1837. "The whole scene since I have been in this country," he wrote, "has been nothing but a heartrending one. . . . If I could, and I could not do them a greater kindness, I would remove every Indian tomorrow beyond the reach of white men, who, like vultures, are watching, ready to pounce upon their prey and strip them of everything they have or expect from the Government of the United States."

Despite General Wool's unwillingness to participate in the Cherokee's inevitable removal, the federal government pressed forward. Still most Cherokees refused to leave their homes. Many stubbornly put their faith in John Ross, certain that their noble chief would find a way out of the forced exodus. After all, wasn't the Treaty of New Echota a fake? Surely, the new president, Martin Van Buren, would recognize that and nullify the agreement? But the Cherokees overlooked the fact that Van Buren had been a staunch supporter of President Jackson. Despite there being a new man in the White House, the U.S. government's policy toward the Cherokees would not change. Increasingly desperate, Ross presented a memorial to the U.S. Senate in February 1838, signed by 15,665 Cherokees, asking that the Treaty of New Echota be reconsidered. The memorial was rejected by a vote of 36 to 10. Soon thereafter, citizens of New York petitioned Congress to reexamine the treaty. Their requests were denied as well. Soon public opinion in the North was so negative that President Van Buren offered to allow the Cherokees two more years to prepare. But most people agreed that the proposal, even if approved by Congress, would resolve nothing. The decision had been made.

In May 1838, General Winfield Scott, a veteran of many American battles, arrived in New Echota, Georgia, to take command of the Cherokee removal. After converting the Cherokee council house into a barracks, he mapped out his strategy. First, he divided the remaining Cherokee nation into three parts—western, central, and eastern districts. Then he ordered his men to construct giant collection camps. Whenever a group of Cherokees had been gathered at each camp they would be led to one of three river ports where federal boats would escort them down the Mississippi to the Arkansas River. That done, he got busy with a proclamation to the Cherokees. It read, in part:

Cherokees! The President of the United States has sent me, with a powerful army, to cause you, in obedience to the Treaty of 1835, to join that part of your people who are already established in prosperity, on the other side of the Mississippi. Unhappily, the two years which were allowed for the purpose, you have suffered to pass away without following, and without making any preparation to follow, and now, or by the time that this solemn address shall reach your distant settlements, the emigration must be commenced in haste, but, I hope, without disorder.

Do not, I invite you, even wait for the close approach of the troops; but make such preparations for emigration as you can, and hasten to this place . . . where you will be received in kindness by officers selected for the purpose. You will find food for all, and clothing for the destitute.

But the Cherokees were hardly treated with the kindness that General Scott had promised. They were forced from their homes on the spot. Often, they weren't even allowed enough time to pack or bring blankets for the trip to the stockades.

General Winfield Scott. A religious man, he appealed to his soldiers to be gentle with the Cherokees, stating: "Every possible kindness, compatible with the necessity of removal, must . . . be shown by the troops." But his orders were largely ignored.

Samuel Cloud was a Cherokee boy who turned nine on the Trail of Tears. The following memory was recounted by his great great grandson:

It is Spring. The leaves are on the trees. I am playing with my friends when white men in uniforms ride up to our home. My mother calls me. I can tell by her voice that something is wrong. Some of the men ride off. My mother tells me to gather my things, but the men don't allow us time to get anything. They enter our home and begin knocking over pottery and looking into everything. My mother and I are taken by several men to where their horses are and are held there at gunpoint.

Evan Jones was a Baptist missionary and friend of the Cherokees. When the whites began to removal process, Jones felt a moral obligation to accompany his congregation to the army camps. Through years of working with the tribe, Jones gained the absolute trust of John Ross. When it came time to move west, Ross named him the assistant conductor of a detachment. The following excerpt is from a series of letters that Jones published in *Baptist Missionary* magazine in 1838 and 1839. This first letter is from Camp Hetzel, written on June 16, 1838.

The Cherokees are nearly all prisoners. They have been dragged from their house, and encamped at the forts and military posts, all over the nation. In Georgia, especially, multitudes were allowed no time to take any thing with them, except the clothes they had on. Well-furnished houses were left a prey to plunderers, who, like hungry wolves, follow in the train of the captors. These wretches rifle the houses, and strip the helpless, unoffending owners of all they have on earth. . . . The poor captive, in a state of distressing agitation, his weeping wife almost frantic with terror, surrounded by a group of crying, terrified children, without a friend to speak a consoling word, is in a poor condition to make a good disposition of his property and is in most cases stripped of the whole, at one blow.

The supposedly orderly removal had quickly devolved to plunder and destruction. Gangs of whites followed the soldiers and grabbed whatever they could. Army wagons filled with supplies for the Cherokees were ransacked. At the homes of some wealthy Cherokees, grave robbers looted family burial grounds in search of buried gold. Children got separated from parents. Captured boys and girls were used as bait to lure their parents from hiding. For some, the pain of leaving behind their homes was too great. John Burnett, the United States private, remembers:

In another home was a frail mother, apparently a widow, and three small children, one just a baby. When told that she must go, the mother gathered the children at her feet, prayed a humble prayer in her native tongue, patted the old family dog on the head, told the faithful creatures goodbye and with a child on each hand started on her exile. But the task was too great for that frail mother. A stroke of heart failure relieved her sufferings. She sunk and died with her baby on her back, and her other two children clinging to her hands.

With the exception of a Cherokee named Tsali, all 16,000 tribe members were rounded into army stockades. The conditions were awful. There were no roofs to guard against the hot sun. Their diet was moldy corn and bacon. Diseases ran rampant, including measles, whooping cough, pleurisy, and various fevers. To make matters worse, many Cherokees mistrusted the army doctors and refused medication. On July 21, the following report on the stricken was delivered to General Scott: "They obstinately refused to take medicine . . . they were all old persons and small children." Death was a daily occurrence. The weeping of relatives and the chants of shamans filled the stockades.

Samuel Cloud remembered it this way:

They lead us to a stockade. They herd us into this pen like we are cattle. . . . The nights are still cold in the mountains and we do not have enough blankets to go around.

Several months have passed and still we are in the stockades. . . . We hear that white men have moved into our homes and are farming out fields. What will happen to us?

My mother, my aunts and uncles take me aside one day. "Your father died last night," they tell me. My mother and my father's clan members are crying, but I do not understand what this means. I saw him yesterday. He was sick, but still alive.

It is now Fall. It seems like forever since I was clean. The stockade is nothing but mud.

As awful as the confinement in the stockades was for Samuel Cloud and the other Cherokees, they had not yet faced the worst. The roundup was only the first phase of the operation. The actual removal was still to come. Somehow, General Scott had to get this ragged collection of 16,000 Cherokees to their new territory 1,000 miles to the west.

An artist's rendering of the Trail of Tears. With their heads bowed and hundreds of miles ahead of them, the Cherokee pushed on.

Five

The First Three Groups Go West

COMPLETED ON JUNE 17, 1838, THE CHEROKEE ROUNDUP TOOK TWENTY-five days. But while many in the Cherokee Nation were still being moved into the stockades, some had already begun the arduous journey west.

The first contingent to leave was led by Lieutenant Edward Deas. On June 6, 1838, about 800 Cherokees piled into 6 flatboats at Ross Landing, Tennessee, and headed down the Tennessee River. Travel was difficult—especially at a set of rapids called "the Suck." Deas wrote in his journal: "The river here becomes very narrow and swift and the banks on either side are rocky and steep." Later he wrote that "it was found impossible to keep her [the boat] in the channel, and in consequence was thrown upon the north Bank with some violence but luckily none of the people were injured although one of the Flats was a good deal smashed."

Progress was slow. After three days the unhappy band reached Decatur where they discovered that the river was impassable. Undeterred,

Deas arranged passage on a railroad—thirty-two cars that could carry half of the group at a time. But while the first group traveled on the train, about one hundred of the remaining Cherokees deserted and tried to make their way back to their homes. Many who stayed turned to the bottle with "much drunkenness resulting." Eventually, Deas managed to get the second group of Cherokees to Waterloo, Alabama, where he boarded them onto a double-decker keelboat. By this point only 489 of the original 800 remained. The number of deserters totaled 311. After a long journey down the Mississippi to the Arkansas River, Deas brought his ragged company into Indian Territory. Miraculously, there were no fatalities among the Cherokees who has stayed with him—in large part because Deas had the good sense to make sure that they had the supplies needed to make such an arduous journey. As Deas recalled in his journal:

I have . . . [issued Cotton] in consideration of their destitute condition, as they were for the most part separated from their homes in Georgia without having the means or time to prepare for camping and it was also the opinion of the Physician of the Party that the health of these people would suffer if not provided with some protection from the weather.

The Cherokees had reached their destination intact. Unfortunately, safe passage would not be guaranteed any of the subsequent parties that made the journey.

The next group, commanded by Lieutenant R. H. K. Whiteley, was not nearly as lucky. The Cherokees were justifiably angry at how they had been driven like cattle from their homes. As a result, many refused provisions and clothing. After a few days on the boat on the Tennessee River, a young child died. Later, an old man died when he tried to retrieve his hat from underneath a locomotive.

As June turned to July, the heat became crippling. A drought took

This coat was worn by a Cherokee man on the hard trip west.

hold in the South—one of the worst in years. Obviously, the severe weather greatly impacted the travelers. As one remembered:

The weather was extremely hot, a drought had prevailed for months, water was scarce, suffocating clouds of dust stirred up by oxen and wagons, and the rough and rocky roads, made the condition of the sick occupants of the wagons miserable indeed. Three, four, and five deaths occurred each day. To avoid the heat the marches were started before sunrise and ended at noon. Before the end of the month there were between two and three hundred ill.

On August 1, the party arrived at Lee's Creek, near Indian Territory. Stopping there, Lieutenant Whiteley took stock of the Cherokee's condition in his journal.

Did not move this day, the party requiring rest and being more than one half sick; notwithstanding every effort used, it was

Legend has it that this Cherokee woman—Walini—was known for singing on the trail to try and alleviate the misery.

impossible to prevent their eating quantities of green peaches and corn—consequently the flu[x] raged among them and carried off some days as high as six and seven.

Of the more than 800 Cherokees who had been with the contingent at the beginning, only 602 arrived in Indian Territory. Some of the remaining two hundred had fled, but most had died en route.

Still, the high mortality rate did not prevent a third group from venturing west that summer. Setting off on June 17, the day the roundup officially ended, 1,070 Cherokees traveled by wagon and foot 160 miles to Waterloo, Alabama. Again, embittered by their harsh treatment, many refused blankets and clothing. One adult and four children died en route. When the group was herded onto flatboats at Waterloo, Nathaniel Smith, the federal agent chosen to oversee the Indian removal, was petitioned by assistant chief George Lowrey and other Cherokee leaders to stop the emigration until cooler weather in the fall. The rivers were too low for travel, they argued. Wells and freshwater springs were dry.

Spare their lives; expose them not to the killing effects of that strange climate, under the disadvantages of the present inauspicious season, without a house or shelter to cover them from above, or any kind of furniture to raise them from the bare ground, on which they may spread their blankets and lay their languid limbs, when fallen prostrate under the influence of disease.

Agent Smith was not moved. He admitted that the Indians "were about naked barefoot and suffering from fatigue." But he also found "their health improving and they well provided with transportation and sustenance." Therefore he gave the order for the march to continue. It was a cruel decision. Indians continued to desert in droves. Many died. Later that summer, Smith himself predicted that, "of the 3,000 which I wrote you from the Agency had left in three parties, not over 2,000 will reach their new home."

With Nathaniel Smith determined to keep the Cherokees moving west, John Ross was in Washington lobbying for a last-minute change in the federal policy. But Ross was overlooking some simple facts. Other native tribes had already met a similar fate. The Choctaws and Chickasaws had been forced to move west, paving the way with their own suffering and deaths. Members of the Creek had resisted only to be defeated in battle. Other Creeks had been persuaded to help ferret out the Seminoles who still maintained a stronghold in Florida swamps. Less fortunate Seminoles were already being sent by boat to the Arkansas Territory. Perhaps it was a case of wishful thinking, but Ross held to the belief that with the Cherokees history would not repeat itself. His tribe would be allowed to stay in the East.

So while Ross was in Washington making this desperate plea, another group of Cherokees decided to take matters into their own hands. On June 17, they penned a letter to General Scott:

> We your prisoners wish to speak to you. . . . We ask that you not send us down the river at this time of the year. If you do we shall die, our wives shall die or our children will die. . . . We want you to keep us in this country until the sickly time is over, so that when we get to the west we may be able to make boards to cover our families.

Scott agreed. No other contingents would leave that summer. The next departure was set for September 1. On July 13, John Ross finally returned from Washington. Though he was unable to get the federal government to relent, he was able to get the War Department to agree to let the Cherokees direct their own removal. General Scott was only too happy to be released from what he viewed as a horrible duty. Many

Charity along the Trail of Tears, *a mural by Brother Mark Elder in the visitors center at the Trail of Tears State Park in Cape Girardeau County, Missouri*

Americans, on the other hand, were outraged that Ross was to be given charge of his people's relocation. After all, the Creeks, Choctaws, and Chickasaws hadn't been afforded such a luxury. Former president Andrew Jackson was especially upset. On August 23, he wrote:

> What madness and folly to have anything to do with Ross when the agent was proceeding well with the removal on the principles of economy that would have saved at least 100 per cent from what the contract with Ross will cost.

I have only time to add as the mail waits that the contract with Ross *must be arrested*, and General Smith left to superintend the removal.

And so as the summer of 1838 drew to a close John Ross was back in Cherokee territory, supervising the removal of his tribe. The Cherokees were to be divided into thirteen parties of about 1,000 people each. Leaders were chosen and routes planned. The cost of removal was estimated at about 16 cents a person per day, or $65.88 for the whole trip. Unfortunately, Congress had not allotted nearly that much for the journey. Finally, the Cherokees had no choice but to pay for the added moving expenses themselves. The extra costs would be deducted from the purchase price of their homeland. The commissioner of Indian affairs found this arrangement acceptable, writing, "As their funds pay for it, and it was insisted on by their own confidential agents, it was thought it could not be rejected."

With General Scott's seal of approval, the exodus was scheduled to begin on September 1. The last party would leave no later that October 20. The Army ordered 645 wagons along with 5,000 horses and oxen. Clothing was purchased, and water transport was arranged for the seriously ill. Ross put his brother Lewis in charge of handling the contracts for wagons, rations, and provisions. About half the money would be used to lease horses. At the last minute, soap was purchased and deducted from the cost of the homelands. They were finally ready.

As for the three parties that had already made the trip, the first contingent, under Lieutenant Deas, arrived in Indian Territory with 489 of the original 800. The second, Lieutenant Whiteley's group, endured a death rate of five a day. When they finally reached Lee's Creek on the edge of Indian Territory, there were 602 out of 1,000 alive. Seventy-two had died. The rest had fled. When the third contingent—the one accompanied by Agent Smith—arrived only 722 remained of the 1,070 who had left Ross's Landing.

As it turned out, Smith's prediction that a third of the Indians would not make the journey turned out to be all too true. Of the three thousand Indians who had left the East, 1,813 arrived safely.

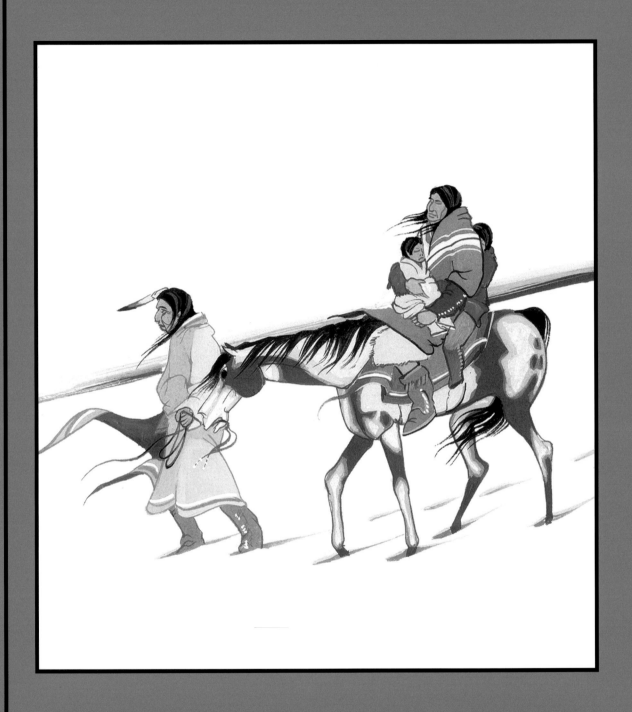

The Cherokees braved extreme cold on their trip west, traveling, according to a traveler from Maine, "on the sometimes frozen ground, and sometimes muddy streets, with no covering for the feet except what nature had given them."

Six

On the Trail

WILLIAM SHOREY COODEY WAS A NEPHEW OF JOHN ROSS. ON AUGUST 28, he witnessed a Cherokee contingent getting ready to depart:

At noon all was in readiness for moving; the teams were stretched out in a line along the road through a heavy forest, groups of persons formed about each wagon, others shaking the hand of some sick friend or relative who would be left behind. The temporary camp covered with boards and some of bark that for three summer months had been their only shelter and home, were crackling and falling under a blazing flame; the day was bright and beautiful, but a gloomy thoughtfulness was depicted in the lineaments of every face. In all the bustle of preparation there was a silence and stillness of the voice that betrayed the sadness of the heart.

Over the period from August 28 to December 5, thirteen groups of Cherokees started for the West. Sadly, the new contingents fared as badly as the first. The drought was over, but only to be replaced by extreme cold. None of the Cherokees had the proper clothing or tents to travel under such frigid conditions. Many divisions trudged through knee-deep mud. Some braved blizzards. Food was scarce. Men would leave to hunt—to supplement the diet of salt pork and flour. Disease ran rampant through the travelers. No one escaped horrible stomach cramps.

One man described passing a bedraggled group of Cherokees "camped for the night by the road . . . under a severe fall of rain accompanied by heavy wind . . . and the cold wet ground for a resting place . . . even aged females, nearly ready to drop into the grave, were traveling with heavy burdens attached to the back."

Theodore Pease Russell lived in the eastern Ozarks in 1838. He remembered the Cherokees this way:

A few days before the Indians came a man arrived to find suitable camping spots and supplies such as corn, oats, and fodder for their teams. There were so few people in the Arcadia Valley then there was only one man who had much to spare.

When I heard the laughter of the boys and girls, I could hardly realize I was in an Indian camp, among people who had been called savages. But I also noticed that many of the old men and women did wear a savage look and seemed as though their hearts were full of hate toward the white race, and they would be glad to take your scalp if it were in their power to do so.

Given what the tribe had been through, it was hardly surprising that many Cherokees would be angry at a white man who dropped by to watch them at their camp. Further, the soldiers who were assigned the duty of escorting the Cherokees west, gave them no reason to be friendly.

General Scott had appealed to the "Christian natures" of the troops, hoping they would treat the natives with "kindness." Unfortunately, the average soldier's treatment of the natives was horrible. Missionary Evan Jones wrote from the trail:

The work of war in time of peace, is commenced in the Georgia part of the Cherokee nation, and is carried on, in most cases, in the most unfeeling and brutal manner; no regard being paid to the orders of the commanding General, in regard to humane treatment of the Indians. I have heard of only one officer in Georgia, (I hope there are more,) who manifests any thing like humanity, in his treatment of this persecuted people.

Of all the firsthand accounts of the Trail of Tears perhaps none is more compelling than that of John G. Burnett, a private in the U.S. Army. Having grown up in Cherokee country, as a boy Burnett was friends with many of his Indian neighbors. Unfortunately, as a young man he was given the assignment of escorting the Cherokees west. His memories of the journey are especially vivid.

The only trouble I had with anybody on the entire journey west was a brutal teamster by the name of Ben McDonal, who was using his whip on an old feeble Cherokee to hasten him into the wagon. The sight of that old and nearly blind creature quivering under the lashes of a bull whip was too much for me. I attempted to stop McDonal, and it ended in a personal encounter. He lashed me across the face, the wire tip on his whip cutting a bad gash in my cheek. The little hatchet that I had carried in my hunting days was in my belt and McDonal was carried unconscious from the scene.

Later, Burnett describes more of what he saw on the trail:

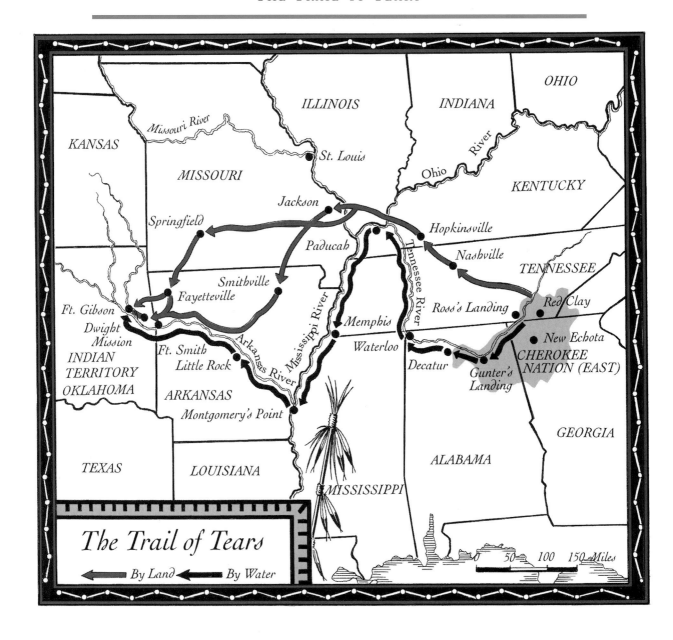

The Trail of Tears

← By Land ← By Water

A map of the routes taken by the Cherokees on their forced march to the Indian Territory.

One can never forget the sadness and solemnity of that morning. Chief John Ross led in prayer, and when the bugle sounded and the wagons started rolling, many of the children rose to their feet and waved their little hands goodbye to their mountain homes, knowing they were leaving them forever. Many of these helpless people did not have blankets, and many of them had been driven from home barefooted.

On the morning of November the 17th we encountered a terrific sleet and snowstorm with freezing temperatures, and from that day until we reached the end of the fateful journey on March the 26th, 1839, the sufferings of the Cherokees were awful. The trail of the exiles was a trail of death. They had to sleep in the wagons and on the ground without fire. And I have known as many as twentytwo of them to die in one night of pneumonia due to ill treatment, cold, and exposure. Among this number was the beautiful Christian wife of Chief John Ross. This noble hearted woman died a martyr to childhood, giving her only blanket for the protection of a sick child. She rode thinly clad through a blinding sleet and snowstorm, developed pneumonia and died in the still hours of a bleak winter night, with her head resting on Lieutenant Gregg's saddle blanket. . . . Her uncoffined body was buried in a shallow grave by the roadside far from her native mountain home in Tennessee, and the sorrowing cavalcade moved on.

The death of John Ross's wife, Quatie, is one of the best-known tragedies of the trip. The child to whom she had given her blanket lived, but she did not. Though she was the wife of a chief her funeral was no different than the four thousand others on the trip. Quatie Ross was laid to rest with no coffin in a shallow, hastily dug grave. After a few quick prayers the party moved on.

The sick and dying were everywhere. As Samuel Cloud recalled:

Quatie Ross, wife of Chief John Ross. The sick child to whom she had given her blanket recovered, but Ross died of pneumonia near Little Rock, Arkansas.

My mother is coughing now. She looks worn. Her hands and face are burning hot. . . . My aunts try to get me to sleep by them, but at night, I creep to her side. . . . When I went to sleep last night, my mother was hot and coughing worse than usual. When I woke up, she was cold. I tried to wake her up, but she lay there. The soft warmth she once was, she is no more.

One Cherokee summed up the march with aching eloquence:

Women cry and made sad wails. Children cry and many men cry, and all looked sad when friends die, but they say nothing and just put heads down and keep on go towards West. Many days pass and people die very much.

As the Cherokees "die very much," back east, the president of the United States, Martin Van Buren, was congratulating himself on a job well done. His secretary of war, Joel R. Poinsett, wrote in late November:

The generous and enlightened policy evinced in the measures adopted by Congress toward that people, was ably and judiciously carried into effect, . . . in every instance with promptness and praiseworthy humanity. . . . It will always be gratifying to reflect that this has been effected, not only without violence, but with every proper regard for the feelings and interests of that people.

It is hard to imagine a report more out of step with reality. But while the president and his secretary of war chose to pretend that the relocation had been executed with "praiseworthy humanity," many other Americans were not as easily fooled. In fact, President Van Buren was deluged with the barbed comments of critics railing against the Cherokee plight. A typical editorial—this one from the December 8 edition of the *Daily National Intelligencer*—argued:

Before we can claim for our Government the credit of having dealt "justly" with the Indians throughout, we must sponge from the tablet of memory the enforcement of a treaty with the Seminoles which the Seminoles never made; the removal of the Creeks from their lands in the face of a solemn covenant; the refusal to fulfill our treaty stipulations with the Cherokees for ten years, and the final enforcement of a treaty to which they never assented, and which never could have been carried into execution but by an armed force which it was in vain for them to contend against.

Meanwhile, the flurry of words did nothing to halt the suffering. On December 20, the *Arkansas Gazette* reported that "owing to their exposure to the inclemency of the weather, and many of them being destitute of shoes and other necessary articles of clothing, about 50 of them have died."

A reporter for *The New York Observer* wrote in late January:

One lady passed on in her hack in company with her husband, apparently with as much refinement and equipage as any mother of New England; and she was a mother too and her youngest child about three years old was sick in her arms, and all she could do was make it comfortable as circumstances would permit. She could only carry her dying child in her arms a few miles farther, and then she must stop in a stranger-land and consign her much loved babe to the cold ground, and that too without ceremony, and pass on with the multitude.

When I read in the President's Message that he was happy to inform the Congress that the Cherokees were peaceably and without reluctance removed—and remember that it was on the 4th day of December, when not one of the detachments had reached their destination; and that a large majority had not made even half their journey, I wished the President could have been there that day in Kentucky with myself, and have seen the comfort and the willingness with which the Cherokees were making their journey.

Though all thirteen caravans eventually reached Fort Smith in Indian Territory, the statistics are astonishing. Out of the 16,000 Cherokees who left the East, at least 4,000 didn't live to see their new homeland. With all the undocumented deaths in the stockades, some scholars put the number closer to 8,000. Whatever the exact figure, so many people passed away on the horrible "migration" that the journey came to be known as the Trail of Tears. And a white flower known as the Cherokee rose was said to bloom where each tear fell to the ground.

Like rain, the tears of anguish fell,
    Sad moments locked in time;
Hoped for sounds from a Mission's bell,
    Were hidden with the promised sign.

As wagons, weighted, marked their way,
    From new Echota to where they close;
Where each tear fell, as some will tell,
    will be seen a Cherokee rose.

—"A Cherokee Rose" by Rick Brown

The Cherokee rose is the state flower of Tennessee.

The seal of the new Cherokee Nation. After years of fighting the federal government, the tribe was forced to accept its fate and resolve their internal conflicts.

Seven

After the Trail

THE "MIGRATION" WAS FINALLY OVER. JOHN ROSS AND APPROXIMATELY 12,000 survivors of the Trail of Tears arrived in Indian Territory by March 1839. Unfortunately, the transition to life in their new homeland was to prove difficult. For it was not long before Ross and his worn-down nation found themselves squabbling with two separate factions of their own tribe. First there was their old nemesis, the Treaty Party, many of whom had moved west in 1835 after signing the Treaty of New Echota. Opposing them was a group of Cherokees known as the Old Settlers who had moved for the East to Arkansas in the early 1800s.

Though the Old Settlers had hoped to settle permanently in Arkansas, twenty years later white frontiersmen pushed them farther west. In 1828, they finally arrived at their permanent home in the Oklahoma Territory. There, this smaller group of Cherokees had developed their own customs and form of government.

As a result, when John Ross arrived in his new homeland, he found himself struggling with the Old Settlers and the Treaty Party for the right to rule his own tribe. Neither group had any intention of submitting to the laws of John Ross and the Eastern Cherokees. In an attempt to work out their differences, the various factions agreed to meet in early June 1839. At that meeting, John Brown, the chief of the Old Settlers, proclaimed: "We cordially receive you as brothers. We joyfully welcome you to our country." But after informing the newcomers they had full rights to vote and run for office, Brown added, "It is expected that you will all be subject to our government and laws until they shall be constitutionally altered or repealed."

Though Ross was encouraged to be welcomed in the Old Settlers' fold, he was not without his concerns. First, he thought it crucial that his own eastern band remain united "for the purpose of settling their accounts with the United States, and for securing certain claims for spoilations." Brown agreed, giving Ross and his people the right to negotiate with the federal government as a separate nation. Then Ross broached the issue that was foremost on his mind: his objections to the Old Settlers' form of government, which gave the newcomers little power. On that matter, Chief Brown wasn't as understanding, telling Ross that no changes could be made in the current government until the following October. But Ross wanted a new constitution drawn up immediately. Annoyed, Brown and the Old Settlers broke off negotiations.

Later, some of John Ross's men held a private meeting. Still furious for the backhanded manner in which the leaders of the Treaty Party had negotiated the fateful Treaty of Echota, they read aloud the passage in the Cherokee constitution that barred the unauthorized sale of Cherokee land. The penalty was death for the guilty parties—in this case the leaders of the Treaty Party, Major Ridge, his son John Ridge, and the first editor of the *Cherokee Phoenix*, Elias Boudinot.

John Ridge, who along with his father, Major Ridge, and Elias Boudinot, paid for his role in the Treaty Party with his life.

When Elias Boudinot joined the Treaty Party, he knew that he would be putting his life at risk:

I know that I take my life into my hands, as our fathers have also done. . . . Oh, what is a man worth who will not die for his people? Who is there here that will not perish, if this great nation may be saved?

Boudinot acted in what he felt was the Cherokee people's interest. But the Eastern Cherokees felt he was a traitor. On the night of June 22, three assassination parties formed. The first, assigned to kill John Ridge, numbered twenty-five men. After surrounding his home at daybreak, three men approached the house and pushed the door open. Moving swiftly past his wife and children, they found Ridge in his bed, held a pistol to his head and pulled the trigger. Amazingly, the gun failed. Ridge woke and struggled. He was dragged to his front yard where he was stabbed repeatedly. Then as his wife and children watched in horror, the men stomped on his body. Miraculously, he survived to be carried inside and die in his wife's arms.

John's father, Major Ridge, and Elias Boudinot didn't survive the revenge killings either. Later that morning, Ridge was shot repeatedly as he rode a horse to visit a sick slave. Boudinot was stopped by four men who claimed they needed medicine. Suspecting nothing, Boudinot agreed to help them. The rest is described by a friend:

He walked but a few rods when his shriek was heard by his hired men, who ran to his help; but before they could come back the deed was done. A stab in the back with a knife, and seven gashes in the head with a hatchet, did the bloody work. In his own view he risked his life to save his people from ruin, and he realized his fears.

Though others were slated for execution, they managed to escape. One of them, Stand Watie, Boudinot's brother, wanted revenge. Though John Ross hadn't known about the assassination plans, Watie and other members of the Treaty Party held him responsible. Likewise, many Cherokees demanded that the murderers be brought to trial. But in the end none of the killers was caught.

In an effort to ease tensions, John Ross and his government passed an act in July 1839 that granted forgiveness to all members of the Treaty Party provided they confess their regret for signing the Treaty of New

Warned that the vigilantes were coming, Stand Watie was the only one who managed to escape being killed for his support of removal. He retaliated by setting fire to the home of his nemesis, John Ross.

Echota and they agree not to run for office for five years. Ross also insisted that the Treaty Party grant a full pardon to any person involved in the Ridge and Boudinot murders. But, the Treaty Party rejected the terms, and mayhem followed. A prominent Ross supporter was murdered by Stand Watie. This was followed by a series of killings, prompting one observer to write, "Murders in the country have been so frequent until the people care as little about hearing things as they would hear of the death of a common dog."

There was a genuine threat of Cherokee civil war. Greatly alarmed, the Old Settlers joined with Ross on September 6, 1839 to draft a new Cherokee constitution that closely resembled the one penned in 1827 in their original homeland. Under the new document, Ross was named principal chief, and the Old Settlers were given several prominent positions. But the new agreement could not erase years of underlying resentments. The federal government did not help either by continuing to recognize and negotiate with all three Cherokee parties. In short, war raged intermittently for the next seven years.

During that time, Ross worked tirelessly for the Cherokee Nation. He planned a school system and a new newspaper. He sought to negotiate a treaty with the federal government that would give the Cherokees ownership of their new western lands and the right to self-government. He also sought payment for the turnpikes, schoolhouses, bridges, and buildings the tribe had constructed in their eastern homeland. In the 1840s the Cherokees established a system of public schools. Two seminaries were built, one for men, the other for women. A new newspaper, the *Cherokee Advocate*, began publication in 1844.

Finally, in 1846, past grievances were set aside and John Ross and Stand Watie shook hands on a binding treaty that pardoned all Cherokees for all past crimes and created one, unified nation. Ross lived out the rest of his life in Washington, D.C., and Philadelphia. Just before he died, at age seventy-five on April 3, 1866, he said:

Students at the Cherokee National Female Seminary . . .

. . . and the Cherokee National Male Seminary in 1851.

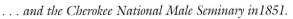

I am an old man, and have served my people and the Govt of the United States a long time, over fifty years. My people have kept me in the harness, not of my seeking, but of their own choice. I have never deceived them, and now I look back, not one act of my public life rises up to upbraid me. I have done the best I could, and today, upon this bed of sickness, my heart approves all I have done. And still I am, John Ross, the same John Ross of former years, unchanged.

After John Ross

JOHN ROSS WORKED TIRELESSLY THROUGHOUT HIS LIFE TO MAKE SURE that his people maintained the right to self-government. Unfortunately, he was fighting a losing battle. In 1887, Congress passed the Dawes Act, a law that divided up land once held in common by Native Americans and allotted it back to them as individuals. When the Cherokees refused, their land was broken up and reassigned to them anyway. In a final effort to retain their sovereignty, the Cherokees and the other four of the original five tribes lobbied Congress in 1905 for the creation of a new Indian state called Sequoyah. The bid was rejected. Instead, the Indian lands were officially disbanded when Oklahoma was admitted to the Union in 1907.

Though the twentieth century has brought the Cherokees their share of hardships, there are currently more than 300,000 of their descendants living in the United States. In 1876, the eastern band of Cherokees—those people who followed Tsali—were awarded 50,000 acres of the Qualla Boundary in present-day North Carolina. Today, nine thousand Cherokees still make their home there and do what they can to keep their native traditions alive. Though most speak English, Sequoyah's syllabary is still taught. They have a strong tribal government, hold elections and publish their own newspaper, the *Cherokee Feather*.

A political cartoon from 1886 shows the Cherokee Nation being tied down, abused by railroad prospectors, U.S. marshals, and the U.S. courts.

After Oklahoma officially became a state, conditions did not improve for the Western Cherokee. Many fell prey to corrupt officials who had themselves appointed as "guardians" to those Cherokees who could not manage their own parcels of land. When oil was discovered in Oklahoma, many of these guardians found ways to assume ownership of the lands they were supposed to be protecting. Kate Barnard, commissioner of Oklahoma's Office of Charities and Corrections, struggled in vain to return the land to its rightful owners:

I have been compelled to see orphans robbed, starved, and buried for money. I have named the men and accused them and furnished the records and affidavits to convict them, but with no result. I decided long ago that Oklahoma had no citizen who cared whether or not an orphan is robbed or starved or killed—because his dead claim is easier to handle than if he were alive.

It was not until the Great Depression of the 1930s that Native Americans were given some relief. In 1933, Franklin Roosevelt passed the Indian Reorganization Act, a law that banned the unregulated sale of Indian lands and that gave money to various native tribes. Thirty years later the Cherokees were awarded 15 million dollars by the federal government in payment for land the United States had forced them to sell in 1893. The Cherokees used this money to build a cultural center. In 1975, the Western Cherokee adopted a new constitution, and in 1984, a joint council met at Red Clay—the site where the Cherokees had met when Georgia first outlawed their government—to reaffirm their cultural heritage.

Modern Cherokees have vowed to never forget the horror of the Trail of Tears. In October 1988, on the one hundred fiftieth anniversary of the removal, more than one hundred men, women, and children gathered at Red Hook Historical State Park, the site of Cherokee Council meetings in the 1830s, to reenact the one-thousand-mile march west. Conditions were difficult. Not only did they travel by horse-drawn covered wagons and mules, the weather was unforgiving. It was often cold, and the roads were slick with ice. But after ten difficult weeks the intrepid group rode into what had been known as Indian Territory. Later that same year, the route they had taken was officially named a National

A Cherokee woman in the 1930s—a member of a new generation of Western Cherokees who most likely never saw their eastern homeland.

Historic Trail by the U.S. government, ensuring that the Trail of Tears would always be remembered. Today the trail is a permanent shrine to the endurance, strength, and dignity of the Cherokee people.

Bibliography

Bial, Raymond. *The Cherokee*. New York: Marshall Cavendish, 1999.

Breyer, Stephen. *The New Republic*, *"For Their Own Good."* Washington, D.C., August 7, 2000.

Brill, Marlene Targ. *The Trail of Tears*. Brookfield, CT: Millbrook, 1995.

Duncan, Barbara R. *Living Stories of the Cherokee*. Chapel Hill: The University of North Carolina Press, 1998.

Ehle, John. *Trail of Tears: The Rise and Fall of the Cherokee Nation*. New York: Doubleday, 1988.

Fleischman, Glen. *The Cherokee Removal*. New York: Franklin Watts, 1971.

Maddox, Lucy. *Civilization or Extinction?* Georgetown University. www.georgetown.edu/departments/amer_studies/limit/maddox.html

Minges, Patrick. *Beneath the Underdog: Race, Religion and the "Trail of Tears."* New York: Union Theological Seminary. www.users.interport.net/~wovoka/underdg7.html

Perdue, Theda, and Michael Green. *The Cherokee Removal—A Brief History with Documents*. New York: St. Martin's Press, 1995.

Perdue, Theda. *The Cherokee*. New York: Chelsea House Publishers, 1989.

Trahant, Mark N. *Picture of Our Nobler Selves*. www.fac.org/publicat/trahant/contents.htm

Further Reading

Bial, Raymond. *The Cherokee*. New York: Marshall Cavendish, 1999.

Brill, Marlene Targ. *The Trail of Tears*. Brookfield, CT: Millbrook Press, 1995.

Duncan, Barbara R. *Living Stories of the Cherokee*. Chapel Hill: The University of North Carolina Press, 1998.

Ehle, John. *Trail of Tears: The Rise and Fall of the Cherokee Nation*. New York: Doubleday, 1988.

Fleischman, Glen. *The Cherokee Removal*. New York: Franklin Watts, 1971.

Perdue, Theda, and Michael Green. *The Cherokee Removal—A Brief History with Documents*. New York: St. Martin's Press, 1995.

Perdue, Theda. *The Cherokee*. New York: Chelsea House Publishers, 1989.

Index

Page numbers for illustrations are in **boldface**.

African Americans. *See* slaves
agriculture, 26, 27, 29
Arkansas, 81
assassinations, 82–86
assimilation, 26

Boudinot, Elias, 40–42, **41**, 47, 83, 84
British, **10**, 17–18
Brown, John, 82
brutality, 17, 18, 30, 58, 72–73
burial grounds, 58
Burnett, John, 7, **8**, 9, 30, 73–75
businesses, 26, 27

Cherokee Nation, 26–27, 30, **80**, 82, 86, **89**
Cherokee Nation v. Georgia, 35
Cherokees, **24**, **53**. *see also* Old Settlers
  dissension, 39–45, 81–88
  in England, **10**
  justice system, 13, 35
  legends, 12, **64**, 79, **79**
  prosperous, 27, **28**, 31, 39, 42
  society, 12–13, 26
chiefs. *See* leaders
Clay, Henry, 45–47
clothing, 29, **63**, 65, 72, 75
compensation, 86, 88, 90
constitutions, 27, 30, 82, 86, 90

courts, 35–37
cultural center, 90

Dawes Act, 88
Deas, Edward, 61–62, 68
deaths, 59, 62, 65, 66, 68, 76–77. *see also* assassinations
  estimate of, 78–79
  of Quatie Ross, 75
desertion, 62, 65, 66
De Soto, Hernando, 15, **16**
disease, 15–17, 58–59, 63–65, 72, 75

Eastern Cherokees, 82, 88. *see also* Cherokees
education, 86, **87**, 88. *see also* language
Emerson, Ralph Waldo, 45
escorts, 61–66, 68–69, 72–73
expansion with honor, 20
explorers, 15–17, **16**
eyewitnesses, 57–59, 71–77, 86. *see also* Burnett, John; newspapers

federal government. *See* governments, federal; Indian agents
French and Indian War, 17
fur traders, 17

Georgia, 25–26, 30–34, 35, 42, 51–52. *see also* New Echota
gold, 30, 32
governments
  Cherokee, 26–27, 30, **80**, 81, 84–86, 88, 90
  federal, 18–21, 25–26, 34, 42, 49, 54, 66–67, 68, 86, 88, 90 (*see also* Indian agents)
  state, 18–20 (*see also* Georgia)
Guess,George, 27–28, **29**

housing, **50**, 51–52, 72, 75
hunger, **53**

Indian agents, 89–90. *see also* Morse, Jedediah; Smith, Nathaniel
Indian Removal Act, 34
Indian Reorganization Act, 90
Indian Trade and Intercourse Act, 20–21

Jackson, Andrew, 34, **36**, 37, 43, 67–68
Jefferson, Thomas, 25
Junaluska (Chief), 34

Knox, Henry, 20–21, **21**

land, 13–15, 18–22, **19**, 25–26, **33**, 35. *see also* compensation; Dawes Act; gold; oil
cession, 27, 32
sale of, 40, 43, 44, 82, 90
western, 86
language, 27–28, 88
laws
Cherokee, 26–27, 32, 40
federal, 20–21, 34, 88, 90
of Georgia, 30–32, 35
leaders, 42–43. *see also* Boudinot, Elias; Brown, John; Lowrey, George; Ridge, John; Ross, John
liquor, 51–52, 62
livestock, 27, 29
looting, 58
Lowrey, George, 65

magazine articles, 11, 12, 57
Marshall, John, 35–37
missionaries, 28–29, 35–36, 48, 57–58, 73
monument, 90–91
morale, 62, **64**, 65, 71, 72, 75, 77
Morse, Jedediah, 27
murals, **67**

New Echota, 43–45, **46**, 49, 54
newspapers, 28, 40–42, 48, 77–78, 86, 88
North Carolina, **19**, 20, 88. *see also* land

northern United States, 34, 45, 54

oaths, 35
oil, 89–90
Oklahoma, 81, 88–90
Old Settlers, 81–82, 86
ownership, 15, 26, 27, 86

Penn, William, 48
Poinsett, Joel R., 77
population data, 79, 81, 88
property, 15, 26, 27. *see also* housing
public opinion, 11–12, 28, 45–47, 48, 54, 67, 77–78

railroads, 62
reenactment, 90–91
religion, 13, 17, 29
relocation, 34, 39–40, 44–47, 52
costs, 68
enforcement, 55
journey, **60**, 61–69, **67**, **70**, 72–73, **74**
roundup, 57–59, 61, 65
route, **74**, 90–91
Revolutionary War, 18
Ridge, John (father), 40, 42–44, **43**, 53, 82, 84
Ridge, John (son), 40, 42–43, 82–84, **83**
right of discovery, 18
Roosevelt, Franklin, 90
Ross, John, **38**, 39–45, 47–49, 54, 57, 66–68, 82–88
Ross, Quatie, 75, **76**

Schermerhorn, John F., 43
Scott, Winfield, 55, **56**, 66–67, 68, 73
Sequoya, 27–28, **29**, 88
Sequoyah (state), 88
settlers. *See* white settlers
slaves, 26, 27, 31
Smith, Nathaniel, 65–66, 68–69
Southern United States, 18–20
survivors
descendents of, 88, **91**
estimated, 79, 81

Trail of Tears, 79, 90–91. *see also* relocation
treaties, 18–20, 21–22, 26, 31, 48, 86. *see also* New Echota
Treaty Party, 40, 42–44, 81–86. *see also* assassinations

Van Buren, Martin, 54, 77
Vann family, 27, **28**

Walini, **64**
Washington, George, 20
Watie, Stand, 84–86, **85**, 86
weather, 62–63, 65, **70**, 72, 75
websites, 92, 93
Western Cherokees, 88–90, **91**. *see also* Cherokees
Whiteley, R. H. K., 62–65, 68
white settlers, 18, 35, 52, 58
Wool, John Ellis, 54
Worcester, Samuel, 22
Worcester v. Georgia, 35–36